Grizzly Bears

by Grace Hansen

Abdo
ANIMALS OF
NORTH AMERICA
Kids

abdopublishing.com

Published by Abdo Kids, a division of ABDO, PO Box 398166, Minneapolis, Minnesota 55439.

Copyright © 2016 by Abdo Consulting Group, Inc. International copyrights reserved in all countries. No part of this book may be reproduced in any form without written permission from the publisher.

Printed in the United States of America, North Mankato, Minnesota.

102015

012016

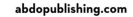 THIS BOOK CONTAINS RECYCLED MATERIALS

Photo Credits: iStock, Shutterstock

Production Contributors: Teddy Borth, Jennie Forsberg, Grace Hansen

Design Contributors: Laura Mitchell, Dorothy Toth

Library of Congress Control Number: 2015941758

Cataloging-in-Publication Data

Hansen, Grace.

 Grizzly bears / Grace Hansen.

   p. cm. -- (Animals of North America)

ISBN 978-1-68080-111-8 (lib. bdg.)

Includes index.

1. Grizzly bear--Juvenile literature.   I. Title.

599.784--dc23

                   2015941758

Table of Contents

Grizzly Bears

Grizzly bears live in North America. They live in parts of the United States. They can be found in Canada, too.

4

Grizzlies live in many **habitats**.
They live in woodlands, forests,
and prairies. They like to be
near rivers and streams.

Grizzlies have thick fur. It
is almost always dark
brown. Some grizzlies
can be light cream or black.

9

Grizzlies eat many foods.

They mainly eat nuts, berries, and other plant parts. Their favorite treat is salmon.

Grizzlies have humps on their backs. The hump is a muscle from digging. Bears have to dig for food. They also dig their **dens**.

Food and Sleep

Grizzlies eat a lot. But they
eat even more before winter.
They have to gain lots of
weight. They do this to
prepare for **hibernation**.

14

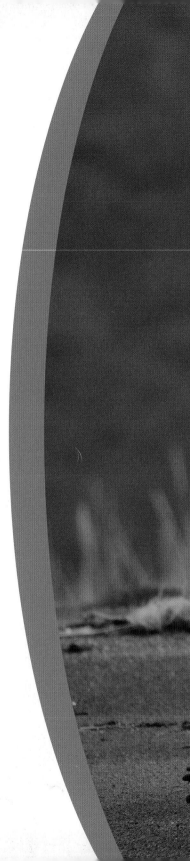

Most grizzlies sleep through

the winter. They sleep in **dens**.

Dens keep them warm and safe.

16

17

Baby Grizzly Bears

Female grizzlies have babies in winter. Baby bears are called cubs. Cubs drink their mother's milk. Mothers don't eat all winter.

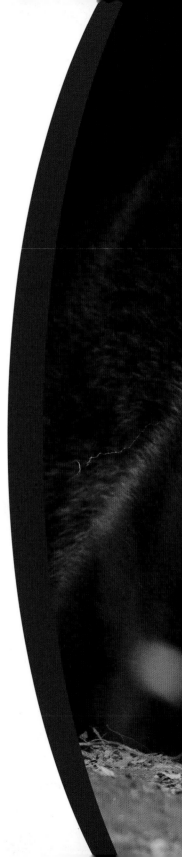

Male grizzlies leave their

dens in March. Females and

cubs wait until April or May.

Cubs are stronger by this time.

More Facts

- In Canada and Alaska, grizzlies are called brown bears.

- Grizzlies prepare for **hibernation**. They eat a lot. They gain about 3 pounds (1.4 kg) per day!

- Grizzlies lose up to 30% of their body weight in the winter.

Glossary

den – an animal's home that is usually underground or on the side of a hill.

habitat – a place where an animal naturally and normally lives.

hibernation – an inactive state that some animals go into to pass the winter months; this state protects them from the cold and lessens the need for food.

Index

abdokids.com

Use this code to log on to abdokids.com and access crafts, games, videos, and more!

Abdo Kids Code:
AGK1118